AS ENDLESS IS MY LOVE AS THIS:

A History of Marriage Rings

Berganza

Antique and Vintage Jewellery

88-90 Hatton Garden London EC1N 8PN

www.berganza.com

Having spent all my working life involved in jewellery, I remain fascinated by the many facets of its entrancing appeal. From mining for gemstones in some of the remotest parts of the world to running a specialist antique and vintage jewellery business in London's Hatton Garden, I have seen this enthralling subject from many different angles.

While I can modestly say I have built up a depth of knowledge over all of those years, I am also delighted to admit that I continue to learn. There is something new to discover about jewellery virtually every day.

Talking to customers, I have also found that there is huge interest in the traditions, myths, history and design of jewellery. It is this that has prompted us to write this book, shedding a little light, I hope, on the development of engagement and wedding rings as we know them today. The choice of an engagement ring is, of course, something which is entirely personal to the couple. If by giving some insight into how engagement rings have evolved over the centuries, recounting some anecdotes about their history and development, and highlighting key figures in their design, it helps them in making a selection today, this book will have served its intended purpose.

An engagement is symbolic. I will be delighted if, after reading this book, couples have an even better appreciation of the extent of that symbolism, giving their chosen ring even more meaning for them.

Paul Daughters
Managing Director

Berganza Ltd

Throughout the span of jewellery history one would struggle to challenge the supreme importance of the marriage ring.

Indeed, it is one of the most significant and treasured objects in a person's life. Nothing, it could be argued, is more valuable – not just for its materials, but for its symbolic and sentimental significance as well. Despite this elevated standing, many of us are unaware of the intriguing and ancient history of wedding rings, both for betrothal and for the marriage itself.

FIGURE 1
Red-figure pyxis by the Meleager Painter,
wedding of Heracles & Hebe,
circa 400-390 BC

ANCIENT GREECE

The oldest known rings clearly associated with love were made in Ancient Greece, although there is no firm evidence of any relating specifically to betrothal or marriage. Examples include rings dating from the Hellenistic era (4th to 1st century BC), bearing inscriptions such as 'beloved' along with a person's name, and cameo and intaglio rings depicting symbols associated with love, such as Aphrodite and Eros, the Greek gods of love. The latter were most likely used as a talisman, or lucky charm, to bring good fortune or protection to the wearer in matters of the heart. Those that may have been related to matrimony take the form of 'Hercules knots', symbolising, according to some scholars, fidelity, to others, the untying of the bride's garments after the marriage. One extremely rare ring (figure 2) is engraved with a couple in a partial embrace, and thus had very possibly been made for a marriage, making it one of the earliest examples of a wedding ring.

FIGURE 2
Greek signet ring
of a man and a woman,
3rd–1st century BC

FIGURE 3
Amorini goldsmithing,
Pompeii, 1st century AD

ANCIENT ROME

Following in the Greek tradition, the Ancient Romans also appear to have worn rings with some aspect of amuletic romantic purpose. Dating from the 1st and 2nd centuries AD, there are numerous examples of Roman intaglio rings engraved with the Greco-Roman gods of love, as well as others representing harmonious relationships, as seen in the example engraved with the god of carnal love and beauty, Cupid (figure 4), and another with the goddess of harmony, Concordia (figure 5), her name literally meaning 'with [one] heart.' Rings with amorous messages were also made, such as that engraved with the word 'AMANIT', meaning 'beloved' (figure 6) dating from the 2nd to the 3rd century AD.

Ever-pioneering, the Romans are widely credited with the invention of the engagement ring. Sometime in the 1st century AD it became customary to hold a betrothal ceremony (called a '*sponsalia*') at which the prospective bride's father or guardian promised her in marriage to the groom. He affirmed his reciprocal pledge by providing his future bride with a ring, called the '*annulus pronubis*'. According to Pliny (23–79 AD), the first betrothal rings were made of iron, but by the 2nd century AD Tertullian (160 – 220) records that gold was preferred by those who could afford it.

FIGURE 4
Roman cornelian signet ring of Cupid, 2nd century AD

FIGURE 5
Roman cornelian signet ring of Concordia, 2nd century AD

Rather than an exchange of rings, the joining of hands (*dextrarum iunctio*) marked the consecration of the marriage ceremony, which explains why some betrothal rings from the 2nd century onwards feature a handshake (the prototype of the modern fede ring, '*fede*' meaning 'faith' in Italian), or a male and female figure facing one another and shaking hands (figure 7), culminating eventually in just a bust-length portrait of a male and female regarding one another. Rings of this type appear either with engraved gold bezels or set with cameos; some are also engraved with words, such as '*omonoia*', meaning 'unity'.

Exactly how such rings were worn is open to speculation. Rather romantically, according to the writer Aulus Gellius (c. 123 – c. 165 AD), the betrothal ring was worn on the third finger of the left hand because a vein from this finger flowed directly to the heart. Pliny relates that the Britons and the Gauls, however, wore wedding rings on the middle finger.

FIGURE 6
Roman signet ring inscribed 'Beloved', 3rd century AD

FIGURE 7
Roman betrothal ring, 2nd-3rd century AD

FIGURE 8
Sarcophagus of the Dioscures, detail depicting a marriage, late 4th century AD

FIGURE 9
Marriage of Emperor Constantine
and Saint Helena, 11th century

BYZANTIUM

During the Byzantine era Christianity came to prominence, and nuptial rings gradually became an integral part of the actual marriage ceremony. Thus it is during this period that we first see the use of three marital rings, rather than one – an engagement ring for the woman and wedding rings for each party, as is the modern tradition. The rings would have been worn together on the third finger of the left hand, this placement being in keeping with the Romans, according to Gellius.

The iconography of Byzantine marriage rings naturally reflects this shift from a secular agreement to a union of two individuals ordained by God. Betrothal rings that integrated the Roman marital handshake remained popular through the early Byzantine era; however, eventually Byzantine rings not only featured overt Christian symbolism denoting the presence of divinity in the marriage – such as a cross (figure 10) or Christ in between the marital couple – but also displayed frontal portrait-like images of the couple, thereby indicating the importance of the individuals themselves in the blessed union. The figures were also typically crowned, a ritual that remains part of the modern Greek Orthodox marriage ceremony.

Although such rings could probably only be afforded by the very wealthy, this provided no impediment to a couple of lesser means, as the following passage by St Augustine (354–430 AD) relates: 'No priest shall hesitate to wed a couple who present themselves before the altar, if the bride and bridegroom are not able, because of poverty, to give rings to each other; for the [offering of] the earnest-money is a matter of decorum, not of necessity.'

FIGURE 10
Byzantine betrothal ring, 6th–7th century

FIGURE 11
Illuminated manuscript, the '*Decretals of Pope Gregory IX*', Giovanni d'Andrea, 14th century

THE MIDDLE AGES

The romantic ideas of chivalry and courtly love were largely formed during the medieval period and resulted in no shortage of love jewellery, including marriage rings. The clasping of hands continued to be part of the engagement ritual, which in England took place at the church door, where maidens were made 'handfast' to their suitor. Thus, stemming from the aforementioned Roman tradition, rings decorated with a handshake, or *fede* rings, were likely types for betrothals. By this time this motif took a fully three-dimensional form, the clasped hands themselves comprising the bezel rather than being depicted in two dimensions, carved on a gem or metal plaque. Some Italian rings as well as pendants and brooches of the 15th century feature a male and a female head gazing at one another, harking back to Byzantine marriage rings.

The hand upon which marital rings were worn seems to have varied during this period. As for which finger, there does seem to be a general preference for the third finger, in accordance with the Ancient Roman idea of the 'love vein' and perpetuated in the early 7th century by Isidore of Seville (c. 560–636 AD): 'The ring is given by the espouser to the espoused either as a sign of mutual fidelity or, more probably, in order to join their hearts by this pledge, and therefore the ring is placed on the fourth finger because a certain vein, it is said, flows thence to the heart,' (at this time the thumb was counted as the first finger).

The spread of the ideals of courtly love, starting in the late 11th century, was in large part due to the French troubadours, or travelling lyrical poets. Thanks to these origins, French became the language of courtly love, and appears on the earliest examples of a new form of love ring, called a 'posy' or 'posie' ring. The name derives from the French '*poésies*', meaning short love poems.

FIGURE 12
Sapphire ring, 14-15th century

The earliest examples, dating from the 13th and 14th centuries, feature inscriptions in French or Latin, typically on the exterior of the band, in capital black-enamelled lettering. Popular phrases were *pense de moy* (think of me), *due tout mon coer* (with all my heart), and *sans departier* (without being parted), to name just a few. In the late medieval period the fashion for posy rings spread to England, and English then became the poetic language of choice. Three charming examples are the wedding rings of the daughters of the Earl of Warwick (d. 1439), with the inscriptions 'Till deithe depart', 'Never newe', and 'Til my live's end'.

Gem-set rings first became popular for marriages and engagements during the medieval period, probably as a result of increased trade with the East, specifically the rich gem sources of India, Ceylon, Persia and Arabia. Diamonds, prized as they are today for their hardness, became fitting symbols of fidelity, although they were not readily available until the 14th and 15th centuries. One early example of an English medieval diamond marriage ring, dated to the 14th century, is set with a single uncut diamond (reflective of the limitations in cutting technology at the time) and bears the inscription '*Sans fine loiaute*' ('Loyalty without end') (Private Collection). Another famous medieval diamond engagement ring was that given by the Archduke Maximilian to Mary of Burgundy in 1477—often considered to be the first diamond betrothal ring.

FIGURE 13
Signet ring of a dog and heart, 15-16th century

FIGURE 14
Incised brass effigy of Robert de Freville and his wife Clarice, circa 1400

Coloured stones were also set in marriage rings during this time. In the will of an Englishwoman from 1503 is listed her 'marrying ring', set with a ruby and a diamond. The inclusion of coloured stones seems to have been popular in the Low Countries as well, as is evident from various contemporary wedding portraits in which brides can be seen wearing such rings. As with diamonds, coloured stones also were given symbolic meanings. Rubies and garnets (often mistaken for rubies, as were red spinels) were popular in love jewellery, as colours redolent of passion were particularly associated with marriage. Sapphires, also a favourite for love rings, were symbolic of marital chastity. There is an example in the Victoria and Albert Museum, London, of a gold and cabochon sapphire ring from this period, certainly a love ring if not an actual marriage ring, with its hoop inscribed 'Love conquers all' and 'Hail Mary' in Latin (M.181-1975); it is much the same in shape and date as the example illustrated on page 13 (figure 12).

In the late Middle Ages another form of love ring appeared, known as a 'gimmel' ring. The name comes from the Latin *gemellus*, meaning 'twin', since it was formed by two interlocking hoops that together made the complete bezel. They very possibly derived from the joining of the engagement and the marriage ring, or were perhaps symbolic of the union of the two lovers. They are often set on one side with a ruby and on the other with a diamond or emerald. Akin to posy rings, they frequently contained a message engraved within the overlapping shanks; many of these referred to the unbreakable bond of Christian marriage as well as citing the names of the couple. Some examples also incorporate the clasped hands of the fede ring.

The use of symbolism in the decoration of marital jewellery also became more varied. Hearts first became popular during medieval times, in addition to lovers' knots or bows, perhaps harking back to the precedent of the Greek Hercules knot ring. The dog was also used as a symbol of fidelity, as seen in figures 15 and 16, the latter example combined with double hearts as well as clasped fede hands at the rear of the shank. Certain flowers and plants came to acquire romantic meanings, and therefore lent themselves to decorative use in marital rings. Ivy, for example, was associated with fidelity, wedded love and friendship.

Concurrently, a custom of using rings as part of the marriage ceremony developed in Jewish culture. One of the earliest references to such a practice was made in the year 1400 by the Rabbi Jakob ha-Levi Mölln, from Mainz in the Rhineland. These rings were purely ceremonial, and took the form of a wide, flat hoop with the bezel fashioned as a small house that probably symbolized the marital home (although others believe it to refer to Solomon's temple, or perhaps the synagogue in general). Furthermore, the metals used represented the coin offered by the bridegroom for the bride, and were not permitted to be set with gems. The earliest known example, found in the Alsace region of France, dates from 1347. In later versions the roof opens to reveal an inscription (such as 'MAZEL TOV'), and they also incorporate filigree and coloured enamel decoration. Such rings continued to be used as late as the 19th century.

FIGURE 15
Signet ring of dog and double-heart bezel, 15-16th century

FIGURE 16
Signet ring with 'fede' shank, 15-16th century

FIGURE 17
Eleanora da Toledo
by Agnolo Bronzino, circa 1543

THE RENAISSANCE

During the Renaissance, marriage rings began to closely resemble those of today, both in use and in form. In Germany and other parts of Continental Europe it became accepted practice for the couple to exchange rings, although not necessarily at the ceremony itself. In England, however, only the woman wore an engagement or wedding ring of any kind.

The finger upon which the ring was to be worn was formally mandated as a result of the English Reformation, when the Edward VI *Book of Common Prayer* (1549) stipulated that the wedding ring should be worn on the third finger of the left hand. On the Continent, however, customs varied. In a portrait of Mary Stuart, Queen of Scots – a Catholic, and born of a French mother – we see her wedding ring being placed on the third finger of her right hand for her marriage to Francis II of France in 1559. In Italy, Spain and the Low Countries it appears there was a trend for wearing the marriage ring on the index finger, as exemplified in both *The Betrothal* by the Flemish painter Lucas van Leyden, dating from the early 16th century, and in *Eleanora da Toledo* (figure 17), Agnolo Bronzino's portrait circa 1543.

Bronzino's painting reintroduces the topic of the diamond wedding ring, one example of which the sitter proudly displays. A highly similar ring can be seen (figure 18), although the stone here is a quartz table-cut in the manner of a diamond, reflecting not only the fashion for but also the scarcity of diamonds. Typical of the period, it demonstrates the shift in focus from metalwork to gemstones in jewellery design. With specific regard to marriage, at around the turn of the 16th century diamonds clearly came to signify eternity – the meaning they retain today – and when set within the circle of a ring, everlasting marital love.

FIGURE 18
Quartz ring, 16th century

A miniature painting of Hymen, the god of matrimony, which was created for the marriage of Costanzo Sforza and Camille d'Aragon in Pesaro in 1475 (figure 20), makes the association very clear. In it Hymen is dressed in a robe decorated with rings set with uncut diamonds, and faces an altar upon which stands a similar ring supported by two burning torches, representative of the betrothed couple.

At this time India was the primary source of diamonds, whence they increasingly made their way westwards courtesy of Arab traders, via Venice, and then on to Bruges, at the other end of Europe's primary trading route. This is where the stones were cut and polished, although the technology of the time only permitted the natural form to be altered in the simplest way, resulting in what is known as the 'table' cut. In this cut, the point of the natural octahedral diamond form is cleaved off, as can be seen from the example gracing Eleanor's finger. Rare and highly prized, they were only affordable to the elite, and primarily the royals of Europe. Mary Tudor (later Mary I) was betrothed as a child to the Dauphin of France in 1518 with a diamond ring. Marguerite of Angoulême received a diamond marriage ring from Henri II of Navarre in 1527, and Anne of Denmark received a 'great ring of gold enamelled set with five diamonds' for her marriage to James VI in 1589. Diamonds were also combined with other stones, often rubies because of their associations with passionate love. As in the Middle Ages, other coloured stones also featured in marriage rings at this time. Emeralds, signifying hope and fertility, and sapphires, for fidelity, were also common in such jewels, most often set as a solitaire or in pairs.

FIGURE 19
Engraved posy ring, 16th century

FIGURE 20
Depiction of Hymen, the divinity of marriage, with a diamond ring and diamond ring cloak, 1475

Plain bands were also used for marriage. One example of a plain wedding band is that of Mary Tudor upon her marriage to Philip II of Spain in 1554. Unlike her childhood betrothal ring (the intended marriage was never to be), Mary's 'marriage-ring was a plain hoope of gold without any stone in it; for that was as it is said her pleasure, because maydens were so married in old Types'.

Posy rings continued to be popular in England, although in the 16th century they changed considerably – they were now characterised by inscriptions appearing on the interior of the band rather than the exterior, as was the previous convention. This was probably for romantic effect, as is indicated by John Lyly in *Eupheus* (1578), when he wrote: 'posies... always next to the finger, not to be seene of him that holdeth you by the hands, and yet know to you that wear them on your hands'. Furthermore, the poems were written in capital letters filled with black enamel, leaving the exterior free to be fancifully engraved and sometimes decorated in coloured enamel. Lady Catherine Grey's wedding ring, dating from 1560, was composed of five interlocking hoops, so that it could contain a lengthy poem, a testament to the acceptance of posy rings as wedding bands. The fashion for both gimmel and fede rings also continued. Like all things Renaissance, designs became more ornate, and often incorporated coloured enamel decoration, including designs such as hearts, turtle doves, garters, and other symbols of fidelity. An example rich in nuptial symbolism integrates table-cut diamonds, a garter and the posy '*L'amour peut tout*' ('Love can do all').

There is some evidence that signet rings began to be used by men as marriage rings during the Renaissance. According to some it became practice in England for the bride to give the groom a ring informally on the day of the wedding ceremony. Mary, Queen of Scots was said to have given her second husband, Lord Darnley, a signet ring upon their marriage in 1565 (now in the collection of the Victoria and Albert Museum, London, M.841-1871), which was engraved with lovers' knots, his initials and the Royal Arms of Scotland. The purpose of this ring, however, has since been called into question. That said, in the same collection is a portrait of a man, dated c. 1540, in which he is holding a carnation – a clear symbol of betrothal in the 16th century – and prominently displaying a large gold signet ring, suggesting that such rings had multiple functions.

FIGURE 21
Marriage of the Virgin
By Raphael, (detail), 1504

FIGURE 22
Buckle posy ring with diamond set buckle-form bezel, 16th century

FIGURE 23
Marriage of Marie de' Medici to Henry IV by Peter Paul Rubens, circa 1622

THE SEVENTEENTH CENTURY

In the 17th century both engagement and wedding rings became increasingly common. By the latter half of the century the tradition was firmly established, as English clergyman Jeremy Taylor attests in *The Marriage Ring* (1653): 'It ties two hearts by an eternal bond, it is like the Cherubims flaming sword set for the guard of Paradise.' As for the wearing of such rings, the *Rituale Romanum* (1614), an official book pertaining to Catholic church services, established that the wedding ring was to be worn on the left hand instead of the right. That said, it seems that they were still worn in various other ways, such as on the index finger (figure 23), the thumb, or on a cord if the ring did not fit (as was often the case with inherited rings). On occasion people even wore two wedding rings, as was depicted in the *Portrait of Izaak Walton* (figure 27), in which he wears two gold bands on his left ring finger, having been widowed and then remarried. Of course, the picture also confirms the fact that there was indeed a custom in England for men to wear wedding rings at this time.

Both gem-set and plain rings were used in the wedding ceremony. Although those set with gems could at first only be afforded by the wealthy, as trade increased so did gem availability. Samuel Pepys, for example, was able to afford a diamond-set wedding ring for his wife. Royalty also favoured diamond marriage rings: Mary of Modena received a diamond-set ring at her proxy marriage to James II in 1673, and the same ring was used at the wedding of their son, James Stuart in 1719; in France, Louis XIV gave the Infanta Maria Teresa of Spain a diamond ring upon their marriage in 1660. However, there is also evidence that the austerity of the unadorned band was sometimes preferred, as can be seen from a portrait of Prince William of Orange and Mary Stuart (Mary II) of England painted in honour of their marriage in 1677; despite her lavish diamond brooch and pearl necklace, she wears a plain gold band.

FIGURE 24
Early old mine diamond and black enamel ring, late 17th century

Diamonds became more popular during this time as a result of increased trade with India, as well as through further advances in diamond cutting technology made over the course of the 17th century. The diamond cutting industry now made its first great strides towards modern cutting practices, incorporating many more facets. The rose cut – a hemispherical form with triangular facets and a flat base – was introduced in the early 17th century; and the first version of the 'brilliant' cut, with a cushion-shaped outline and kite and triangular-shaped facets, appeared around 1660.

Unlike today, diamonds were often set in rings that had intricate enamel decoration. This was quite colourful in the early 17th century, a holdover from Renaissance taste. There was a marked shift towards a preference for diamonds with black enamel in the second quarter to the latter half of the 17th century, as seen in figure 24, which is also remarkable for being set with an old mine cut diamond. This contrast of white and black was characteristic of the baroque style, and indeed it can be seen in most of the arts of Europe at this time, not just jewellery and fashion. Despite the increased popularity of diamonds, however, coloured stones were still prized in marital jewels, especially rubies for their associations with love, and emeralds, symbolic of hope and childbirth. They frequently appear in fede and gimmel rings of this period, often paired with diamonds and heart shapes to further emphasise the marriage symbolism.

Notwithstanding the relative increase in the availability of gemstones, more economical modes of decoration were common in marriage rings. Band rings were most often plain, but could also be decorated with intricate enamelled engraving. Although the fragility of enamel has meant that these rings very rarely survive intact today, such decoration can be seen in figure 27, which incorporates the fede motif on the exterior of the band, and is said to have been made for a wedding by the family in which the ring has remained since its creation. A ring that had the same motto was advertised as lost in 1659, under the description: 'ring which was a wedding ring tied with a black ribbon...with a lock of hair in it and the poesie *United hearts death only parts.*'

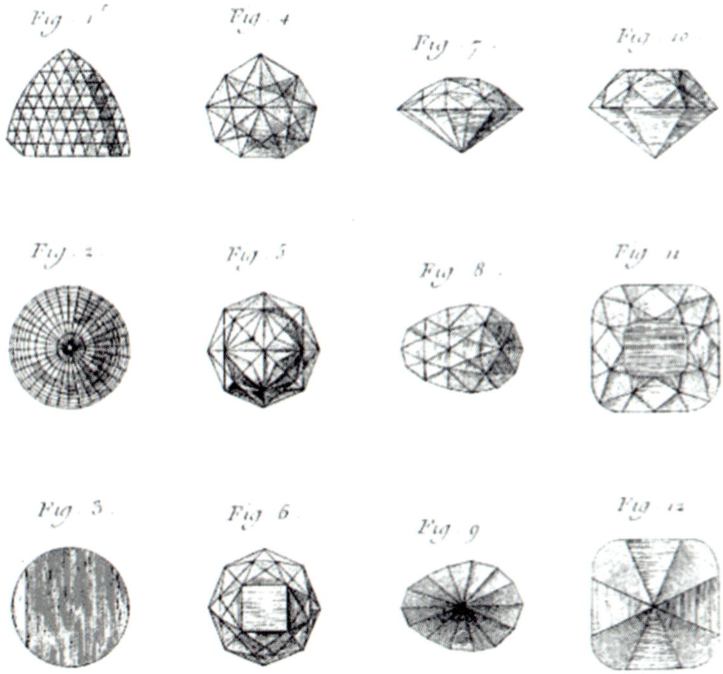

FIGURE 26
Early diamond cuts, from '*Encyclopédie*', Paris: Chez Briasson, 1751-1776

FIGURE 25
Heraldic bloodstone signet ring, 17th century

Posy rings were probably the most widespread wedding jewel of this century, and often bear clear nuptial messages – for example, 'I have obtained whom God ordained' (see figure 28). They can be separated from earlier versions by a shift in the middle part of the 17th century from capital lettering in black to lower-case italic script, a trend that lasted through the early 19th century. Posy rings were so popular, in fact, that books of mottos were published for the aid of jewellers and clients alike, which explains why many posy rings are inscribed with the same mottos. Some clients were more creative, however, as in the instance of Samuel Pepys, who recorded that he and his family sat around the fire composing posies for his son's impending nuptials.

It would seem that heraldic rings were also used as wedding rings. These naturally lent themselves to marital union, since they often depicted the combined coats of arms of the husband and the wife – for example, the joining of the Waterhouse and Willis families proclaimed in figure 25 is denoted by the arms 'impaled' (the term for the combination of two coats of arms). Another fine example is a German signet ring in the Victoria and Albert Museum, London (M.229-1975) that bears the two initials of the bride and groom, two clasped hands around a bunch of forget-me-nots – a symbol of true love – and the date, 1634.

FIGURE 27
Enamelled posy ring,
late 17th century

FIGURE 28
Engraved posy ring,
17th century

FIGURE 29
Izaak Walton by Jacob Huysmans, circa 1672

FIGURE 30
Queen Charlotte by
Sir Thomas Lawrence, 1775

THE EIGHTEENTH CENTURY

By the 18th century the modern usage of marital rings was firmly established – if the couple had the financial means, the bride received both an engagement and a wedding ring, and the groom a wedding ring as well. The wearing of marriage rings on what is today known as the 'ring' finger of the left hand, at least in Western Europe and the Americas, was also widespread, as is reflected in the portraiture of the day.

Jewellery of this first part of the century was inspired by the florid and ornate rococo style, and in the latter half of the century by the symmetry and austerity of Classical antiquity. As a result, marriage rings in the early part of the century are marked by delicacy, as manifested in openwork designs with scrolling ornamentation. Diamonds were still paramount among the love stones, helped by an increase in their availability after a major discovery of diamonds in Brazil in 1727. The combination of these two factors resulted in larger openwork bezels set with floraform clusters of diamonds. Rings such as figure 31 and figure 32 were used as marital rings, the former very similar to an example engraved with a pair of initials and a date, and therefore probably a marriage ring, from the Alice and Louis Koch Collection (cat. 881).

Solitaires still remained popular, although now they were often flanked by smaller diamonds at the shoulders. The ultimate trend-setter of her day, Queen Charlotte (1744–1818) received a diamond solitaire engagement ring from King George III in 1761, which is probably the one she wears in a portrait by Sir Thomas Lawrence of 1775 (figure 30). This she protected with what was called a 'keeper' ring – a band ring worn on the outside of the diamond solitaire, which was engraved with the date of the wedding, and can be considered to be the precursor to today's eternity band.

FIGURE 31
Open work diamond ring, early 18th century

FIGURE 32
Diamond cluster ring, late 18th century

Hers was lavishly set all around with a single row of diamonds, as is figure 33, of a similar date. She was, after all, known at the time as the 'Queen of Diamonds'.

Aside from the plain solitaire diamond ring, perhaps the most popular design was that of a heart or pair of hearts between two hands, often surmounted by a crown or lovers' knot, variations of which can be seen here (figure 34). Three-stone rings, like figure 32, were most likely a simplification of the image of two hands holding a heart. As is evident from each of these examples, diamond cuts were quite irregular at the time, and although cutting technology continued to advance, rose cuts remained popular. The combination of rubies and emeralds with diamonds remained fashionable as well, owing to their appropriate marital symbolism. Two new yet related types of marriage rings appeared at this time – portrait rings, containing a miniature portrait of the groom (among her many wedding jewels, Queen Charlotte received one of these as well), and cipher rings, bearing the new monogram of the bride, typically in diamonds on deep blue enamel, encircled by diamonds.

Posy rings continued to be popular as wedding and love rings throughout the 18th century. Examples abound and become quite regular. One nice example (figure 36) reads 'We Joine our hearts in God'; judging from its large size, it was a man's wedding band. However, around the turn of the century posy rings finally fell from fashion, possibly due to new laws that required the interiors of band rings to be marked with various assay and hallmarks.

FIGURE 33
Diamond guard ring,
18th century

FIGURE 34
Diamond, emerald and ruby
crowned double heart ring,
18th century

FIGURE 35
Mr and Mrs Ralph Izard
by John Singleton Copley, 1779

FIGURE 36
Posy ring, 18th century

FIGURE 37
The Royal Family by Franz Xaver Winterhalter, 1846

THE NINETEENTH CENTURY

As the use of both engagement and wedding rings was firmly established, marriage rings took on myriad new forms during the 19th century. This diversity was largely influenced by growing demand: the Industrial Revolution had given rise to the new middle class, and as a result such items became more affordable to a greater number of people. As in the medieval period, with its embracing of the ideals of courtly love, the 19th century saw the emergence of a similar movement in Romanticism, beginning in about 1820 and pioneered by artists who promoted the use of any form of love token, including nuptial jewels.

Queen Victoria was paramount among those who promoted sentimentality, and was a particular lover of Romantic jewellery, as can be seen from her marital rings. The Queen received a snake-form engagement ring in 1839, which she wore in many of her portraits (figure 37, The Royal Collection, London); the head of the serpent was set with an emerald (similar to the one illustrated in figure 38, save the ruby). The snake represented eternity, and the emerald, along with its traditional symbolic connotations of fertility and good luck, was also her birthstone. Such whimsical forms are found throughout Victorian jewellery. Her wedding band, however, was plain, and in turn she gave Albert a plain gold band on their wedding day.

FIGURE 38
Ruby and diamond snake ring, circa 1900

FIGURE 39
Diamond cluster ring, late 19th century

Despite Victoria's emerald ring, the diamond engagement ring continued to grow in popularity, not least because of the discovery of diamonds in South Africa in 1867. This made the gem more accessible to people from a greater range of income levels. The firm establishment of the diamond engagement ring in the zeitgeist of this era is reflected in various publications, Robert Tomes' book on etiquette, The Bazar Book of Decorum (1873), being just one example:

The proposition being made and accepted, a ring, called 'the engagement ring,' usually containing a single diamond, of the highest value to which the generosity and means of the giver are capable of attaining, is presented by the successful suitor to his betrothed, who wears it ostentatiously on the ring-finger of her right hand.

Various forms of diamond rings abound, including solitaires, diamond cluster rings (figure 39) and half-hoops set with single or multiple rows of stones (figure 40). Also around this time, what is now widely considered to be the quintessential engagement ring was born. This setting was new in that it raised the diamond up off the shank, supported by individual claws, which allowed light to enter into the stone from all sides (figure 41); this was in contrast to closed-back, collet settings that predominated earlier in the century. That said, the gypsy setting was also quite popular, in which the diamond was set flush into a heavy shank (for example, figure 43).

FIGURE 40
Diamond half-hoop ring, late 19th century

FIGURE 41
Antique solitaire diamond ring in gold by Emile Viener, English, late 19th century

FIGURE 42
Illustration from Charles Dickens' *David Copperfield*, by Hablot K. Browne, 1850

In this age of romance and sentimentality, the language of precious stones was more important than ever, and this was naturally reflected in wedding jewellery of the day. Not only were certain stones symbolic of various aspects of love, but they were also used acrostically, to spell out words of special meaning (a concept invented by the Parisian jeweller Mellerio in 1809). In addition to her wedding ring, Queen Alexandra, consort to Edward VII, Victoria's eldest son and successor, wore a guard ring with coloured stones – beryl, emerald, ruby, tourmaline, jacinth, emerald – whose initial letters spelt 'Bertie', the name by which Edward was known to his family. George Kunz, the pre-eminent gemmologist of the day – employed by Tiffany & Co. – also recorded that such rings were used for engagements. Some of the most common words to be spelt out in this way were 'regard', 'dearest', 'adore', 'forever', and 'love me', 'regard' spelled out in this example (figure 44). As in times before, rubies, emeralds and pearls, the latter symbolic of purity, were often set into engagement rings, and combined with other love symbols such as hearts and lovers' knots (figures 45, 46).

In addition, the symbolic language of plants and flowers was widely popularised by both French and English publications of the middle of the century, and so feature in wedding jewellery designs of the day. Most common are forget-me-nots (symbolic of pure love), daisies (loyal love) and ivy (long-lasting love)— the latter can be seen on the gentlemen's wedding band pictured in figure 47. Men also continued to wear signet rings as a marital symbol. The example seen in figure 48 bears the heraldic shields '*accolée*', or overlapping, in contrast to the impaled arms of the 17th century example.

FIGURE 43
Diamond and sapphire 'Gypsy' ring, late 19th century

FIGURE 44
'Regard' ring, mid-19th century

FIGURE 45
Pearl double-heart ring, late 19th century

FIGURE 46
Emerald and ruby double-heart ring, late 19th century

FIGURE 47
Wedding band engraved with hearts and daisies, late 19th century

FIGURE 48
Heraldic amethyst signet ring, late 19th century

FIGURE 49
Princess Elizabeth and Philip
Mountbatten, 1947

THE TWENTIETH CENTURY

'The solitaire diamond as large and as perfect as [the groom] could afford has for many years been the standard engagement ring.' So wrote Ethel Frey Cushing, in her book *Culture and Good Manners*, published in 1926. Technological advances in diamond cutting as well as metallurgy would have a dramatic effect on the jewellery of the early 20th century, perhaps most notably on the diamond ring, which was now firmly established as *the* engagement jewel.

Diamond cutting reached a new level of precision with the introduction of the 'modern brilliant cut', based upon the mathematical optimisation of light and its reaction with the stone to maximise brilliance and fire. New shapes also came into fashion, such as the emerald, pear, marquise and baguette cuts. Developments in the working of platinum resulted in the production of more delicate, strong, untarnishable white metal mounts, which suited these new uniform diamond cuts. As a result, particularly in the first two decades of the century, designs became gem-centric, the mounts with intricate detailing.

From First Lady Eleanor Roosevelt, who received a Tiffany diamond solitaire in 1903, to the Queen (then Princess Elizabeth), who was given a diamond ring with diamond-set shoulders, the stones having been once set in a tiara belonging to Prince Philip's mother, Princess Andrew of Greece, in 1947, diamond engagement rings abound throughout the first half of the 20th century.

FIGURE 50
Boucheron marquise diamond ring with tapered diamond shoulders, French, circa 1950

FIGURE 51
Flanked solitaire diamond ring, circa 1920

FIGURE 52
Wedding ring advertisement,
C. D. Peacock, 1928

This trend was further encouraged by the introduction of the famed De Beers slogan, 'Diamonds are Forever' in 1948. Although by this point diamond engagement rings had become a centuries-old tradition, it seems that this had a strong effect on Prince Rainier III of Monaco: he first gave his bride-to-be Grace Kelly a ruby and diamond eternity band from Cartier in honour of their engagement, but when he learnt of the trend for diamond solitaires, he gave her a twelve carat emerald-cut solitaire diamond ring. The 20th century was also the age of famous designers, who stamped their own style on the now classic form of the diamond engagement ring.

Despite the popularity of the diamond ring, coloured stones remained among the top choices for engagement rings. Around the turn of the century the crossover design, influenced by the scrolling motifs central to the Art Nouveau movement, presented itself as an ideal engagement jewel. These were often set with a diamond and another precious stone, such as an emerald, a ruby, sapphire or pearl in platinum-topped yellow gold (figure 54). Seaman Schepps, New York jeweller to the stars, gave his wife a diamond and opal crossover ring upon their engagement in 1910. Another famous crossover engagement ring was the diamond and emerald ring by Van Cleef and Arpels given by John F. Kennedy to Jacqueline Onassis in 1953.

FIGURE 53
Sapphire and diamond crossover ring, circa 1910

FIGURE 54
Diamond and ruby crossover ring, circa 1910

Coloured stones on their own were also widely fashionable. The Duke of Windsor, for example, gave Wallis Simpson an engagement ring by Cartier set with an extremely fine 19.77 carat emerald. Some of the new Hollywood glitterati of the 1930s and '40s also preferred coloured stones – William Powell, for example, gave Jean Harlow a large cabochon sapphire engagement ring in 1937. But perhaps the most famous engagement ring of the 20th century is the sapphire and diamond cluster ring by Garrard (similar to figure 55), that belonged to Diana, Princess of Wales and then served as the engagement ring of the Duchess of Cambridge.

As for wedding rings, however, the old-fashioned plain gold band persisted as the classic choice. In his book of 1917, George Kunz of Tiffany remarked: 'Although a diamond ring is the one most appropriate as an engagement ring, it has long been recognised that for a wedding ring nothing can replace the simple hoop of precious metal, which may, indeed, be rendered a trifle less plain by some very chaste and beautiful engraving.' While gold remained the preferred metal for most, new materials and decorations emerged, perhaps the most popular being platinum, plain or finely engraved. He commented that platinum made a fitting symbol of eternity since it does not tarnish.

For those with more lavish tastes, the eternity band was the wedding ring of choice. As noted in a 1938 issue of Vogue, then and today the arbiter of fashion, 'What better emblem of unending devotion than eternity rings?' Upon Princess Marina of Greece and Denmark's marriage to Prince George, Duke of Kent, in 1934, she received three eternity bands – one in sapphires, one in diamonds, and one in rubies, to represent the colours of the Union flag, nearly identical to the set shown in figure 56. Not to be confined by tradition, Marilyn Monroe wore a diamond eternity band set with thirty six baguette-cut diamonds highly similar to figure 57 as a combination engagement and wedding ring for her whirlwind wedding to the famous baseball player Joe DiMaggio in 1954, reflecting the 20th century penchant for individuality.

FIGURE 55
Sapphire and diamond
cluster ring, circa 1905

FIGURE 56
Set of ruby, diamond
andw sapphire
eternity bands, 1939

FIGURE 57
Diamond eternity band,
circa 1935

From the simple band of iron the Ancient Romans used for betrothals, to the diamond and platinum eternity engagement-wedding ring of Marilyn Monroe, marriage rings have undergone a remarkable evolution over the last two millennia. Yet despite this long history, essentially they are unchanging, ever symbolic in both form and in materials, the perfect physical manifestation of eternal marital love. Surely the giving of marriage rings is a tradition which will continue into this millennium and beyond.

Bury, Shirley. *An Introduction to Rings*, Maryland: Stemmer House, 1984

Campbell, Marian. *Medieval Jewellery in Europe: 1100–1500,* London: V&A Publishing, 2009

Chardour, Anna Beatriz. *Rings: The Alice and Louis Koch Collection,* Leeds: W.S. Maney and Sons Ltd, 1994

Cherry, John. *Medieval Goldsmiths*, London: British Museum Press, 2011

Church, Rachel. *Rings*, London: The Victoria and Albert Museum, 2011

Collings, Olivia and Dawes, Ginny Readington. *Georgian Jewellery: 1714–1830,* London: Antique Collectors Club, 2007

Evans, Joan. *English Posies and Posy Rings*, London: Oxford University Press, 1931

Fasel, Marion and Proddow, Penny. *With this Ring: The Ultimate Guide to Wedding Jewelry*, New York: Bulfinch, 2004

Hindman, Sandra. *Toward an Art History of Medieval Rings: A Private Collection,* Chicago: Paul Holberton Publishing, 2007

Jones, William. *Finger Ring Lore*, London: Chatto and Windus 1877

Kunz, George. *Rings for the Finger*, New York: Dover Publications Inc., 1917

Levi, Karen. *The Power of Love: Six Centuries of Diamond Betrothal Rings*, 1988

Markowitz, Yvonne J. Artful *Adornments: Jewelry from the Museum of Fine Arts, Boston,* Boston: MFA Publications, 2011

McCarthy, Kieran. '*Posy Rings', Antique Collecting; the Journal of the Antique Collector's Club,* May 2011

Munn, Geoffrey. *The Triumph of Love: Jewelry 1530–1930,* London: Thames and Hudson, 1993

Oman, Charles. *British Rings: 800–1914,* London: B.T. Batsford Ltd., 1974

Victoria and Albert Museum: *Catalogue of Rings 1930,* Ipswich: Anglia Publishing, 1993

Phillips, Clare. *Bejewelled by Tiffany: 1837–1987,* London: Yale University Press, 2006

Jewellery from Antiquity to Present, London: Thames and Hudson, 1996

Rudoe, Rudoe. 'Queen Charlotte's Jewellery', *The Wisdom of George the Third,* London: Royal Collection Publications, June 2004

Ruseva-Slokoska, Ljudmila. *Roman Jewellery: A Collection of the National Archaeological Museum – Sofia*, London: Cromwell Editions, 1991

Scarisbrick, Diana. *Rings: Jewelry of Power, Love and Loyalty,* London: Thames and Hudson, 2007

Scarisbrick, Diana and Henig, Martin. *Finger Rings: from Ancient to Modern,* Oxford: Ashmolean Museum, 2003

Tait, Hugh, ed. *7000 Years of Jewellery*, London: The British Museum Press, 2008

Vail, Amanda and Zapata, Janet. *Seaman Schepps: A Century of New York Jewelry Design,* New York: The Vendome Press, 2004

Victoria and Albert Museum Online Museum Catalogue, May 2010

Vikan, Gary. 'Art and Marriage in Early Byzantium', *Dumbarton Oaks Papers,* Vol. 44 (1990), pp. 145–163

FIGURE 1
Red-figure pyxis by the Meleager Painter, wedding of Heracles and Hebe, circa 400-390 BC, K18.1 Theoi Project

FIGURE 3
Amorini goldsmithing, Pompeii, 1st century AD, ALI215428, Bridgeman Art Library

FIGURE 8
Sarcophagus of the Dioscures, detail depicting a marriage, late 4th century AD, British Museum – Ad Meskens

FIGURE 9
Marriage of Emperor Constantine and Saint Helena, 11th century, Medievalists

FIGURE 11
Illuminated manuscript, the 'Decretals of Pope Gregory IX', 14th century, 42-31947224 Corbis

FIGURE 14
Incised brass effigy of Robert de Freville and his wife Clarice, circa 1400, Monumental Brass Society

FIGURE 17
Eleanora da Toledo by Agnolo Bronzino, circa 1543, XIR176269, Bridgeman Art Library

FIGURE 20
Depiction of Hymen, the divinity of marriage, with a diamond ring and diamond ring cloak, 1475, Urb.lat.899, Vatican

FIGURE 21
Marriage of the Virginby Raphael (detail), 1504, BEN33457, Bridgeman Art Library

FIGURE 23
Marriage of Marie de' Medici to Henry IV by Peter Paul Rubens, circa 1622, XIR17690, Bridgeman Art Library

FIGURE 26
Early diamond cuts from 'Encyclopédie', Paris: Chez Briasson, 1751-1776, GIA

FIGURE 29
Izaak Walton by Jacob Huysmans, circa 1672, NPG1168, National Portrait Gallery

FIGURE 30
Queen Charlotte by Sir Thomas Lawrence, 1775, NG4257, The National Gallery

FIGURE 35
Mr and Mrs Ralph Izard by John Singleton Copley, 1779, BST189951, Bridgeman Art Library

FIGURE 37
The Royal Family by Franz Xaver Winterhalter, 1846, 405413, Royal Collection Trust © Her Majesty Queen Elizabeth II 2013

FIGURE 42
Illustration from Charles Dickens' David Copperfield by Hablot K. Browne, 1850, XJF396008, Bridgeman Art Library

FIGURE 49
Princess Elizabeth and Philip Mountbatten 1947, BE072620, © Bettmann/Corbis

FIGURE 52
Wedding ring advertisement, C.D. Peacock, 1928